Australian Geographic

DISCOVER

VENOMOUS ANIMALS CONTENTS

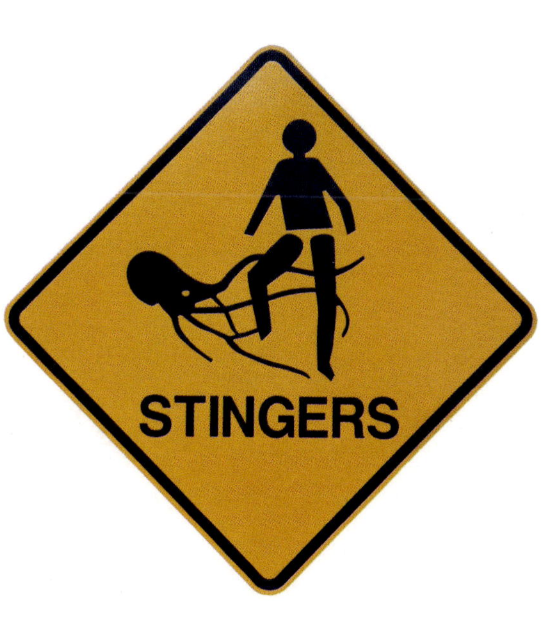

WHAT IS VENOM?

Did you know that animals ooze? Even humans create fluids and slimes known as SECRETIONS. Spit is a secretion, and so is ear wax. Animals make these icky substances for many reasons. Some even make poisons, which contain TOXINS. Some of these poisons, we know as VENOM.

Poisons are meant to make other animals sick – not because the animals making them are mean, but so they can protect themselves or catch a meal. Many toxins work only when a predator eats a poisonous animal.

MULGA SNAKE

VENOM DELIVERY

Some people say venom isn't poison. Don't believe them. It is! But venom is a *special* type of poison. Venomous animals deliver their poison by biting, stinging or piercing the skin of other animals. They inject it using a **VENOM DELIVERY SYSTEM**, whether that is a fang, a stinger or something else.

Scientists sometimes argue about which animals are truly venomous. In this book, we say that any animals (and maybe even some plants) that deliberately inject other animals with toxic fluids are venomous.

GIANT BULLDOG ANT

TARGETED TOXINS

Venom is common in the animal kingdom. Its use is known as its *function*. The function of venom is to scare off, injure, subdue or kill other creatures, and sometimes to help animals snatch a snack.

A venomous creature, such as the giant bulldog ant, is the 'producer' of the venom, and its 'target' is usually its prey, its predator, or its competitor. Luckily, humans are rarely targeted. If they can, most venomous creatures – even those that can make humans sick – would rather get away than attack a human.

DID YOU KNOW?

More than 200,000 venomous species exist! Venom has evolved many times in many types of animals, suggesting it is a most excellent survival skill.

CORAL RABBITFISH

GREENING'S FROG

Many fish, including the coral rabbitfish, have spines that deliver their venom. Venomous snakes and spiders have fangs. Some mammals have spurs. And stingers and sea jellies have barbs or tentacles. Some venomous frogs, such as Greening's frog, even have horns or tusks they use to stab their targets!

SUPER SNEAKY

Venom is like a superpower for the animals that make and deliver it. Often, venomous critters aren't big or strong. Their venom lets them overpower prey or frighten off attackers much bigger than they are.

Parasites may use venom to secure a meal without being detected. Blood-eating ticks, mosquitoes and leeches use their venom to reduce the pain of their bites, letting them feed unnoticed. Their venom also contains toxins that thin the blood and stop it from clotting, making it easier for these parasites to suck it up!

DON'T BELIEVE THE HYPE

Australia is famous for its dangerous animals. We have venomous snakes and spiders, as well as non-venomous predators such as sharks, crocodiles, and … drop bears, oh my! (Of course, the last one is a joke). But is Australia really full of dangerous creatures that are out to get us?

BEES STING FOR DEFENCE.

Venomous animals live all over the world, and most of them are venomous insects (such as bees and wasps), arachnids (such as spiders, ticks and scorpions) or marine INVERTEBRATES. This book is full of 'creepy crawlies' from the land and oceans. They may not be the first animals you think of when you hear the word venomous, but they are all fascinating. Nature is wild!

TIGER SNAKE

DID YOU KNOW?

Australia is the only continent where venomous snake species outnumber non-venomous species, yet our snakes actually bite very few people each year.

TOXIC TRAITS

Venoms aren't simple substances. Imagine a fluid that has 'bits' – like pasta sauce with chunky vegetables in it. Venoms and other secretions also contain bits called **MOLECULES**. Toxins are the molecules in venom that cause changes in the bodies of target animals.

The world is made of molecules – even the purest water is full of them because it is made of molecules, too. Whatever you hear, chemicals aren't all bad. We're all made up of chemical molecules!

Proteins are the most common type of toxic molecules found in venom. They are a special type of molecule that does all sorts of things inside the animals that make them – and sometimes inside other animals, too!

BLUE-RINGED OCTOPUS

Some of the toxins in the venom of the extremely venomous blue-ringed octopus are not proteins, but these octopuses are just a weird exception.

MILKING A SNAKE

Venom is usually made and stored in special tissues or organs known as **GLANDS**. When a venomous critter injects its target, toxins in its venom stop molecules or proteins in the target's body from doing important tasks. Some stop blood from clotting, some are brutal hole-punchers that damage cells, and others can cause **PARALYSIS**, heart failure and even death.

DID YOU KNOW?

Snakes are sometimes 'milked' for their venom. The venom's chemical make-up can be studied to help create antivenom, which neutralises the toxins.

LITTLE NIPPERS

Snakebite must always be treated as a life-threatening emergency. Luckily, Australian hospitals have medicine known as **ANTIVENOM** for treating snakebite. In some ways, Australia is the 'lucky country' when it comes to snakes because many of our deadliest species, such as the inland taipan, live in places where they're rarely seen. In some parts of the world, cobras and other venomous snakes bite people much more often.

MONOCLED COBRA

INLAND TAIPAN

STINGY THINGIES

Venomous animals have existed for a very long time. Among the oldest are jellyfish (which aren't really fish so are often called 'sea jellies'). Their relatives – corals, anemones and hydrozoans – are all cnidarians (tip: the c is silent), but let's just call them all 'stingers'!

Stingers have one of the most spectacular ways to deliver venom. Their special stinging cells, called **NEMATOCYSTS**, have just one job – stinging! Inside each cell is a tiny harpoon. When it is stinging time, the nematocysts explode, and the harpoon shoots out into the target, injecting it with venom.

Stingers have been around for at least 580 million years and maybe more than 700 million years! Stinging must be a very useful trick indeed!

Stingers are found worldwide, and there are tens of thousands of species. All are venomous, but most stings just make the skin tingle, go numb, or break out in itchy welts. Others, such as the box jelly or irukandji, can kill, so pay attention to signs warning about them.

SEA JELLY STINGERS

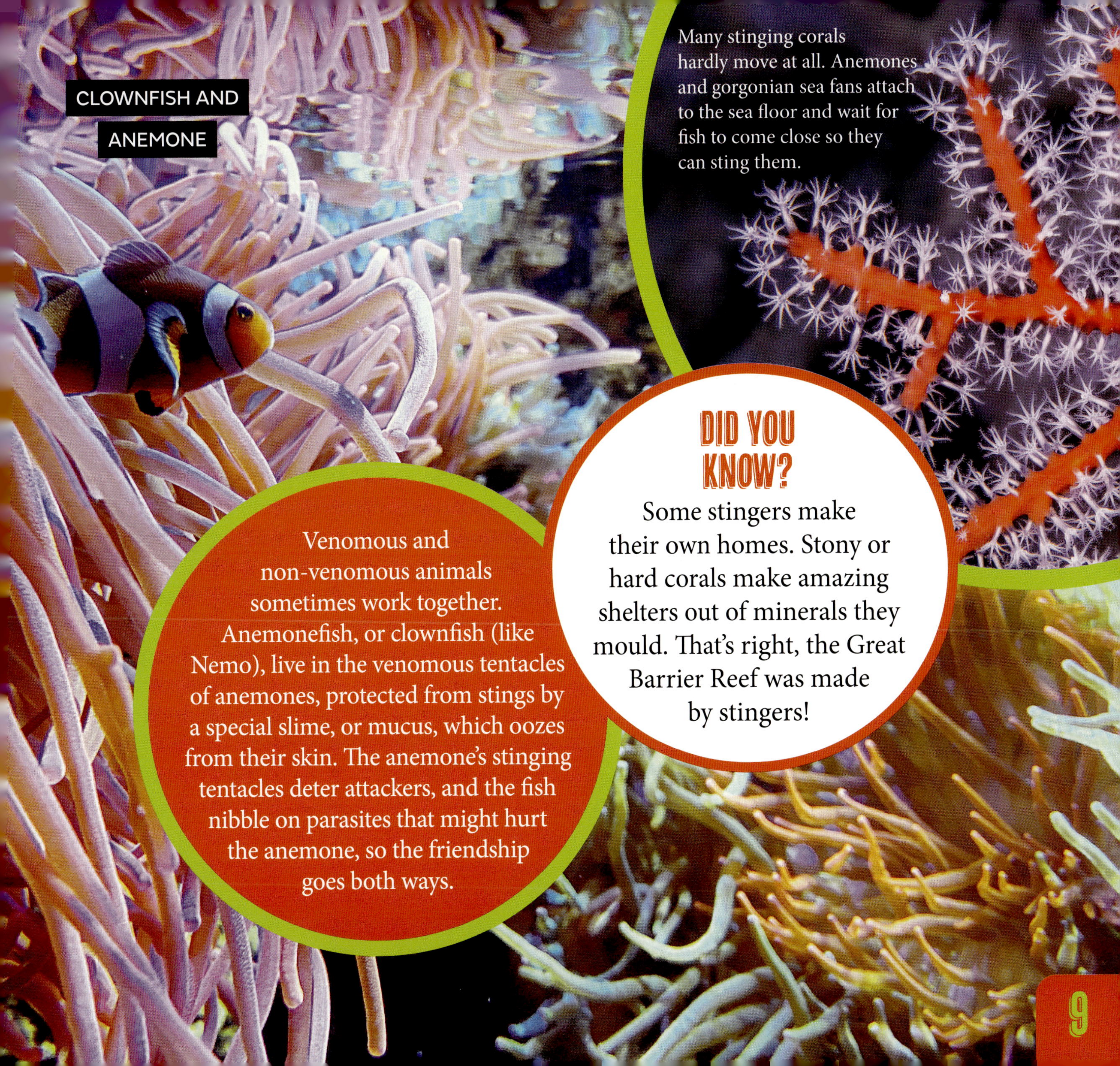

CLOWNFISH AND ANEMONE

Many stinging corals hardly move at all. Anemones and gorgonian sea fans attach to the sea floor and wait for fish to come close so they can sting them.

DID YOU KNOW?

Some stingers make their own homes. Stony or hard corals make amazing shelters out of minerals they mould. That's right, the Great Barrier Reef was made by stingers!

Venomous and non-venomous animals sometimes work together. Anemonefish, or clownfish (like Nemo), live in the venomous tentacles of anemones, protected from stings by a special slime, or mucus, which oozes from their skin. The anemone's stinging tentacles deter attackers, and the fish nibble on parasites that might hurt the anemone, so the friendship goes both ways.

BLACK & BLUE

Some very dangerous stingers wash up on northern Australian beaches in summer. These cnidarians belong to a class called 'cubozoans' (or cube animals), but they're better known as box jellies or sea wasps.

DID YOU KNOW?

If you get a box jelly sting, wash the skin in vinegar right away. An antivenom is also available for sea wasp stings.

Deadly cubozoans include the large box jellyfish and two tiny species – the irukandji, and the common kingslayer. They are excellent reasons to stay out of tropical waters in summer.

Irukandji are tiny and have super potent venom that can kill rapidly.

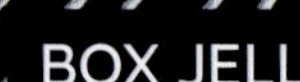

BOX JELLY

Box jellies are strong swimmers that feed on fish and small marine animals they paralyse with their venom.

BLUEBOTTLE

WAR JELLIES

A famous stinger in Australia is the bluebottle, which is known elsewhere as the Portuguese man o' war. It may look like a sea jelly, but it's actually four smaller animals working so closely together that they're easily mistaken for a single animal. Bluebottles can't swim, but they can sail across the ocean, riding the winds.

SPOTTED SEA JELLY

VENOM STEALERS

Animals that eat venomous critters can sometimes survive their venom. The blue dragon sea slug, a type of nudibranch, loves snacking on a bluebottle and even steals its stinging cells for its own use. Never touch a beautiful blue dragon or you could be stung by a cell stolen from a bluebottle. The violet blanket octopus is also a thief. It steals whole tentacles from bluebottles to use as weapons!

BLUE DRAGON SEA SLUG

DEADLY DEFENDERS

Bees, ants and wasps make up one of the largest groups of venomous animals, with more than 150,000 venomous species. Even stingless bees and ants are descended from species that could once sting.

Bee venom is only meant to be painful enough to stop a bee's predators, but some humans are allergic to it, which is why bees kill more Australians every year than snakes do.

BUMBLE BEE

Most bees live in colonies of workers, drones and a single queen. Together, they act almost like a 'super organism'. When the colony is at risk, workers become defending soldiers that sting any threats, giving their lives to protect their queen and their baby siblings in the hive.

When a bee stings, its stinger breaks off with the venom gland attached! It may get stuck in the skin of the attacking predator, while the gland continues to pump in venom.

NATIVE BLUE-BANDED BEES CAN STING BUT RARELY DO

Many wasps are predators that use venom to help them catch prey. But some are sneakier. Some wasps are **PARASITES** that take over the nests or bodies of other animals. You may think these 'zombie' parasites are the stuff of nightmares … but for wasps, taking over and killing a host is just another way to survive.

AN ICKY 'EGG-SPLOSION'

When it stings a caterpillar, the orange caterpillar parasite wasp injects its own eggs along with its venom! This wasp's poison is not meant to hurt or kill the caterpillar. Instead, the wasp's venom stops the caterpillar's immune system from noticing the eggs planted under its skin, letting the eggs develop inside the caterpillar's body and eat its flesh until they get so big they explode through the skin. Ewww!

Other parasitic wasps do use their venom to paralyse target animals. Many of them target spiders. Scientists don't always have great imaginations, so we call these 'spider wasps'. The orange spider wasp uses its venom to paralyse large spiders, such as huntsmen or tent spiders. The unlucky spider is then dragged into a hole in the ground where the wasp lays its larva (another word for the grub-like stage of baby insects) on top of its very own supply of fresh meat – yikes!

BLOODSUCKERS

MOSQUITO

Venomous vampires are all around us! Blood is full of nutrients, and wherever there are animals, there's blood. No wonder so many venomous animals see blood as a free feed.

DID YOU KNOW?

Mosquitoes arc the world's deadliest animals. Like other 'vampires', they pass on blood diseases, such as malaria, in their saliva, along with toxins that stop blood clotting.

The Australian paralysis tick lives on bandicoots, possums and other marsupials. It's not picky, but it is tricky (and 'ticky', too). Ticks use toxins to make sure their hosts don't feel them biting. They make a NEUROTOXIN – a toxin that affects nerves – to make their bite feel painless so they can stay attached to their hosts for days, injecting venom to ensure they stay hidden. To combat this, some marsupials evolved special grooming claws to remove ticks and parasites from their fur.

A KANGAROO WITH TICKS

If you bushwalk in rainforests, you might find a leech on you. They're not dangerous, but their bites can itch because leech spit contains toxins that thin the blood, making it flow better so it is easier to drink.

TOOTHED TERRORS

Some bats are vampires, too. Australia doesn't have actual vampire bats, but the common vampire bat of North America has saliva loaded with toxins that make the blood flow straight into its hungry little mouth! The Australian ghost bat is sometimes called a 'false vampire bat', but it's not really venomous and it doesn't drink blood. It is a fierce predator of small animals, though!

The lamprey looks like a scary giant leech, but it lives in the ocean. Its saliva contains all sorts of toxins – some of which may help scientists make new medicines.

ODDLY VENOMOUS

What has a bill like a duck, lays eggs like a bird, has fur like an otter, and makes milk like a mammal? A platypus, of course. When scientists in England first saw the platypus, they thought it was a fake! They also didn't realise that male platypuses are among the world's few venomous mammals.

Venomous mammals are quite rare, and the platypus is one of the cutest. Along with vampire bats and the platypus, there are venomous shrews (sort of like scary mice) and the slow lorises of Asia.

PLATYPUS

Slow lorises live in South-East Asia and look a bit like cuscuses or monkeys. They make toxins from glands on their arms. Lorises are literally 'armed' with toxins!

SLOW LORIS

Male platypuses have a sharp spine, or spur, on their rear ankles. This venom delivery system connects to a venom gland. Platypuses don't use their venom to catch food but rather to sting other males when they fight during breeding season. Like most venomous critters, they also use their venom to defend themselves, so never pick up a platypus! Their stings are agonising, although they are not life-threatening.

DID YOU KNOW?

Although venom is rare in mammals today, some biologists believe venomous spurs, like the male platypus's, were much more common in mammals in the past.

Platypuses are egg-laying mammals known as MONOTREMES. Their monotreme relatives the echidnas also have spurs, but they're no longer connected to venom glands. This tells us that modern echidnas lost this trait as they evolved, maybe because they are spiny enough to stay safe without them.

SPINE TIME

Spines are a common way to deliver venom, especially for defence. Many fishes, rays and marine invertebrates have venomous spines, and some land-living invertebrates do too.

LIONFISH

The lionfish, in the scorpionfish family, is native to Indo-Pacific waters. It is popular in aquariums for its dramatic colours, but being spiked by its venomous dorsal spines can cause paralysis and changes in heartbeat and blood pressure.

Most spiny fish aren't deadly, but venomous scorpionfishes (a group that includes stonefish and lionfishes) can be. As their name suggests, stonefish are superbly camouflaged to look like rocks on the sea floor. Australia's estuarine stonefish is common across northern Australia. It has hard spines connected to large venom glands, and its stings are torturous and can be deadly, so it is a good thing antivenom is available.

ESTUARINE STONEFISH

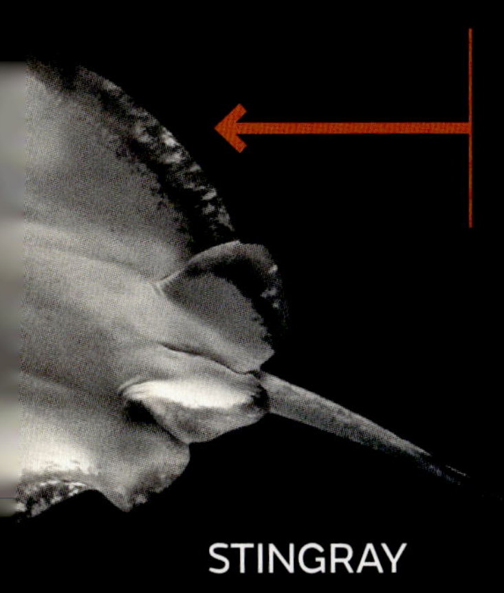

STINGRAY

Stingrays are commonly seen venomous critters. Their spines are at the base of the tail and are used only to defend themselves. Watch where you step if you are walking barefoot in shallow water.

CUPMOTH CATERPILLAR

They may look a lot like spiky marine worms, but cupmoth caterpillars are spiny, venomous moth larvae that live on land. The mottled cupmoth has especially complex venom that contains more than 150 separate toxins!

A THORNY ISSUE

Many ECHINODERMS – a group of marine invertebrates that includes starfish and sea urchins – have venomous spines that can injure other marine life and even humans. The crown-of-thorns sea star is the world's second-largest starfish. It grows up to 50cm wide and sometimes reproduces rapidly in Australia, where it is can destroy coral reefs by eating up to 10m^2 of coral each year.

SEA URCHIN

CROWN-OF-THORNS SEA STAR

DID YOU KNOW?

A crown-of-thorns sea star eats by 'spewing' its stomach out of its body and using it to cover corals. Chemicals made by its stomach then break corals down into a digestible soup. Yuck!

SHARP SHOOTERS

Snails may seem fragile, despite their protective shells, but sea snails are much tougher than garden snails. Some can even be seriously toxic. When a small creature is deadly to much larger animals, venom is often the reason.

Cone snails are among the most venomous critters on the planet, although they are easily mistaken for harmless shells. Mostly, their venom is for killing marine worms, but some grow big enough to eat fish and can even sting humans if we're foolish enough to pick them up. A cone snail delivers its venom with an amazing weapon – a modified tooth that it shoots out of its shell like a harpoon. The tooth is loaded with deadly venom made by a special gland.

GEOGRAPHY CONE SNAIL

DID YOU KNOW?

The geography cone makes two venom cocktails – one for predators and one for prey! Its defensive venom has toxins that make this snail deadly to humans, so make sure you don't touch it!

GEOGRAPHY CONE SNAIL

BLUE-RINGED STINGERS

Snails and octopuses don't look much alike, but they're both molluscs. You can think of octopuses as super-smart snails with eight legs and a shell on the inside. Like cone snails, blue-ringed octopuses are venomous. Unlike snails, they don't make their own venom – or not all of it. They make some of their own toxins, but scientists believe blue-ringed octopuses get their most powerful nerve-attacking toxins from tiny creatures living in their saliva glands. That may be why blue-ringed octopus venom varies so much.

LESSER BLUE-RINGED OCTOPUS

Lots of venomous critters have bright colours that warn they're deadly. Blue-ringed octopuses flash electric blue rings when threatened.

The greater blue-ringed octopus lives across most of South-East Asia and northern Australia. The lesser blue-ringed octopus inhabits southern Australian waters and is sometimes called the southern blue-ringed octopus. Bites from blue-ringed octopuses are very rare, as these beautiful, shy creatures do their best to be left alone. As both of these species live in tidal rockpools, you should be careful where you put your fingers and feet when you're wading at the beach.

GREATER BLUE-RINGED OCTOPUS

HUNTERS &

Most spiders are venomous, but few are a real threat to humans. Spiders are either hunters that track down or ambush their food, or trappers that make webs to catch creatures which blunder into them. Net-casting spiders combine these tactics to throw their nets over their prey!

A JUMPING SPIDER EATING AN INSECT

DINNER TO GO

Spider venom is mostly used to subdue prey and to start digesting it even before a spider ingests it. It sounds gross, but that's what our spit is for, too. Saliva breaks down molecules in food while we chew. Why wait until it hits your stomach?

WHITE-TAILED SPIDER

WEBS OF WONDER

Web-building is a remarkable feat that we often take for granted. Some spiders, such as the garden orb-weaver, take down their web every morning and build a new one each night! Golden orb-weavers, which are not related, build stronger webs and sit in them all day and night waiting for prey to fly in.

REDBACK SPIDER WITH EGGS

TRAPPERS

GARDEN ORB-WEAVER

Garden orb-weavers avoid the risk of being eaten by birds by hiding away during the day.

FUNNEL-WEB SPIDER

Australia's most famous spiders are the funnel-webs. These spiders are thought to be the world's most dangerous. Funnel-web bites have killed 13 people in the past, although no one has died since antivenom was developed in the 1980s.

DID YOU KNOW?

Male funnel-webs have more toxic venom than females. The opposite is true for redback spiders, in which the female is deadlier than the male and even eats him during mating!

NET-CASTING SPIDERS

Net-casting spiders are also called 'ogre-faced spiders' because some look a little scary. They are only mildly venomous and pose no risk to humans. These spiders hang upside down to hunt, dropping their rectangular silk nets over unsuspecting insects that pass below.

PINCH & STING

Scorpions are ARACHNIDS that are related to spiders and ticks. These predators are well-armed. They not only have a venomous sting in their tails but also have pinchy pincers to hold prey while they sting it.

The male Flinders Ranges scorpion has a longer tail and is more venomous than the shorter-tailed (but larger-pincered) female.

Scorpions sometimes eat their own kind. Over time, some evolved more powerful stings, reducing their need for very large pincers. Others evolved powerful pincers and didn't need such a potent sting. This means that the most venomous scorpions often have the weakest pincers.

Despite their fierce reputation, female scorpions are caring mothers that carry their babies on their backs to keep them safe.

RAINFOREST SCORPION

The rainforest scorpion (left) has strong pincers and a tiny tail. The marbled scorpion (below) is the opposite, with a long tail and small pincers. The rainforest scorpion is a popular pet because its sting is weak and it rarely uses it. The sting of a marbled scorpion is very painful, but it isn't deadly.

MARBLED SCORPION

The name 'centipede' means '100 legs', but most centipedes have about 30 – one pair for each body segment. Some, however, have more than 300! All centipedes are venomous, injecting their venom by using special front legs that look like fangs. These legs are called MAXILLIPEDS, which means 'mouth-foot'!

MAXILLIPEDS

LOADS OF LEGS

The giant centipede is Australia's largest centipede species, reaching more than 20cm in length. It is a fearsome predator of frogs, lizards and small mammals. It even eats cane toads.

Centipedes give painful stings, but they aren't really dangerous to humans. Some have very beautiful colours, and one – *Orphnaeus brevilabiatus* from Asia – can even glow in the dark!

GIANT CENTIPEDE

DID YOU KNOW?

Like spiders and scorpions, centipedes shed the outer layer of their skin, known as their 'exoskeleton', as they grow.

SNAKES ALIVE!

Baby brown snakes make different venom to their parents. Babies eat lizards, but adults eat rodents, so their venom changes as they grow. Baby brown snake venom attacks the nerves, but adult brown snake venom attacks the blood as well.

Australia is famous for its venomous snakes, and we certainly have a lot of them! Mind you, even the most dangerous species rarely bite people unless they get stepped on or feel cornered.

Australia's most famous snakes are also our most venomous – taipans, brown snakes, tiger snakes, death adders and black snakes. Brown snakes in the genus *Pseudonaja* are common in Australia. They dine on rats and mice, which are plentiful wherever people live. Because they encounter humans more often, they cause more snakebite deaths than other venomous snakes. Mind you. they also control pests, so it is best to leave them alone and stay out of their way.

RED-BELLIED BLACK SNAKE

EASTERN BROWN SNAKE

VENOMOUS & ENDANGERED

The broad-headed snake is a threatened species that lives only in sandstone habitats close to Sydney. It is rare because our suburbs have slowly taken over its habitat and people have removed or damaged the sandstone it lives in. Human actions can cause the deaths of a lot of snakes. Perhaps they think of us as deadly killers!

BROAD-HEADED SNAKE

COLLETT'S SNAKE

DID YOU KNOW?

The inland taipan is often said to be the world's most venomous snake. It does have very potent venom – mostly to rodents! So far, no human deaths from the bite of an inland taipan have been recorded.

INLAND TAIPAN

Many of Australia's venomous snakes aren't well known. Some of these reptiles, such as Collett's snake, the yellow-faced whipsnake, the red-naped snake and the golden-crowned snake, are quite beautiful.

VITAL VENOM

When people think about venomous animals, they often think of danger. But venomous animals can also be a source of life-saving medicines. Because toxins interfere with systems inside human or animal bodies, studying them helps researchers learn a lot about bodily processes.

Bites and stings from venomous animals can be painful, or even deadly, but these animals mostly act in self-defence.

CAUTION!

Remember that any bites from snakes and funnel-web spiders or stings from box jellies or blue-ringed octopuses must be treated as life-threatening emergencies. If bitten, call 000 and get to hospital as quickly as possible!

FUNNEL-WEB SPIDER

Some natural toxins make excellent medicines. Some drugs have already been developed from venomous animals. A blood pressure medication made in 1981 was based on a toxin from the venom of the Brazilian viper.

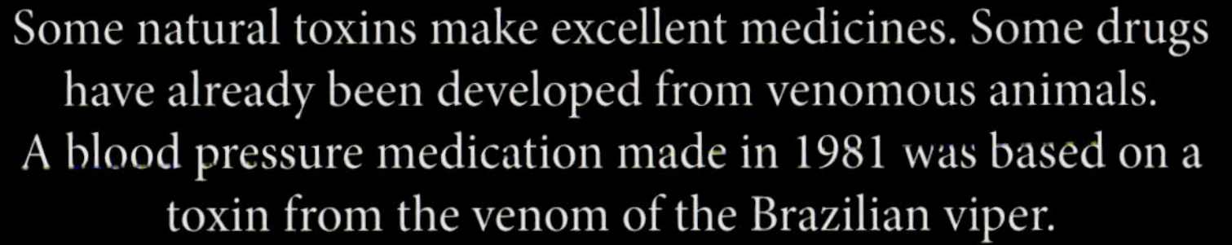

VENOM RESEARCHERS AT AVRU

CONE SHELL

BRAZILIAN VIPER

DID YOU KNOW?

One day, you might be prescribed a drug based on cone snail toxin to control pain, or a medicine based on funnel-web toxin might save your life after a heart attack!

TOXINS HELP US RESEARCH NEW MEDICINES

Researchers from the Australian Venom Research Unit (AVRU) at the University of Melbourne – including this book's author, Dr Timothy Jackson (above left) – study the evolution and composition of many types of venom. They do this to help find antidotes and medicines that can prevent injuries or deaths from envenomation (and because venomous animals are really cool). Of course, the best way to avoid being stung or bitten is to treat all animals with respect and never try to harm them. If you're lucky enough to see venomous creatures in the wild, be sure to admire them from a distance.

GLOSSARY

ANTIVENOM
A treatment that neutralises venom.

ARACHNIDS
Animals in the class Arachnida, such as spiders and scorpions.

ECHINODERMS
Spiny sea creatures in the phylum Echinodermata.

GLANDS
Special organs or tissues that make and store secretions.

INVERTEBRATES
Animals that lack a backbone but usually have an exoskeleton.

MAXILLIPEDS
Modified legs near the mouth of a centipede that are used for feeding, clasping, or injecting venom.

MOLECULES
The smallest unit of a substance in chemistry.

MONOTREMES
Mammals that lay eggs.

NEMATOCYSTS
The stinging cells of cnidarians, which shoot out tiny harpoons.

NEUROTOXIN
A toxin that affects the body's nerve cells.

PARALYSIS
When you can't move your body parts.

PARASITES
Animals that live in or on a 'host' species, making it less healthy.

SECRETIONS
Substances made by a cell, gland or organ of the body and discharged for a specific function.

TOXINS
The molecules that make venom harmful.

VENOM
A special type of poison that gets injected.

VENOM DELIVERY SYSTEM
A body part capable of injecting venom, such as fangs, spines, barbs, spurs or tusks.

PICTURE CREDITS

Images are listed clockwise from top left unless specified. AG = Australian Geographic; SS = Shutterstock.com; US = Unsplash.com; CP = CanvaPro

Front cover: YANN-HUBERT/CP; Ken Griffiths/SS; Ian Scott/SS; SChantra/SS; Vaeenma/Dreamstime; Gena Melendrez/SS; I Wayan Sumatika/SS; Vac1/CP; Carlos Jared/Wikimedia Commons; Ken Griffiths/SS. **1:** naomi tamar/US; Johan Larson/Dreamstime; Ken Griffiths/SS; THP Creative/SS; Andrew Burgess/SS. **2:** Kristian Bell/SS. **3:** Johan Larson/SS; Ian Scott/SS; Carlos Jared/Wikimedia Commons. **4:** ChameleonsEye/SS; Montchak/CP. **5:** xiSerge/Pixabay; David Clode/US. **6:** Marchu Studio/SS; Thierry Eidenweil/SS. **7:** nynkevanholten/CP; Dr Timothy NW Jackson AVRU; David Clode/US. **8:** Pavlo Burdyak/SS. **9:** Kal Rivero/Pexels; unterwegs/SS. **10:** Nick Rains/AG; Lisa-ann Gershwin/CSIRO. **11:** Manja Wiepcke/Pixabay; Pawel Kalisinski/Pexels; Sahara Frost/SS. **12:** Erik Karits/US; Jenny Thynne/Flickr. **13:** Tom/iNaturalist; Craig Taylor/SS; Jenny Thynne/Flickr. **14:** Jimmy Chan/Pexels; Studio Bros/SS. 14–15: Mironmax Studio/SS. **15:** Roberto Dani/SS; Mendesbio/SS; Gena Melendrez/SS; Yutthasart Yanakornsiri/SS. **16:** Slowmotiongli/Dreamstime; Seregraff/SS. **17:** slowmotiongli/CP; Enguerrand Blanchy/US. **18:** Kletr/SS. **18–19:** Benny Marty/SS; Arunee Rodloy/SS. **19:** Graham Wise/Flickr. 20–21: Oksana Golubeva/SS; Juriah Mosin/SS. **21:** YURSAN ABDUL RAHMAN/SS; DiveIvanov/SS. **22:** Muhammad faishol husni/SS; Esther Beaton/AG. 22–23: Dr Timothy NW Jackson AVRU; RealityImages/SS. **23:** Dirk Kaas/SS; Robyn Butler/SS; reptiles4all/SS. **24:** Heather Ruth Rose/SS; Vision Wildlife/SS; David McClenaghan/CSIRO. **25:** I Wayan Sumatika/SS; wk1003mike/SS; THP Creative/SS. **26:** John Carnemolla/SS. 26–27: Kristian Bell/SS. **27:** Ken Griffiths/SS; GoodFocused/SS. 28: Ken Griffiths/SS. 29: Dr Timothy NW Jackson AVRU; Murilo Mazzo/SS; Jack Pokoj/SS; Ivan Samkov/Pexels. **30:** Paul Looyen/SS;. **31:** Denish Doukhan/Pixabay**. Back cover:** Erik Karits/US.

Australian Geographic

DISCOVER

Australian Geographic *Discover: Venomous Animals* is published by Australian Geographic. All text is copyright © Australian Geographic and may not be reproduced without the written permission of the publishers.

First published in 2023
© Australian Geographic Holdings Pty Ltd
52–54 Turner St, Redfern, NSW

editorial@ausgeo.com.au
australiangeographic.com.au

ISBN: 978-1-922388-94-0

Author: Dr Timothy N. W. Jackson
Commissioning Editor: Karin Cox
Creative Director: Aleksandra Beare
Designer: Paul Hodge
Editor: Michele Perry
Print production: Andy Franks

AUSTRALIAN GEOGRAPHIC
Managing Director: David Haslingden
Licensing and Publishing Manager: Tom Bates
Commercial Assistant: Felicity McManus

Printed in China by Leo Paper Products Ltd.
The paper in this book is FSC® certified. FSC® promotes environmentally responsible, socially beneficial and economically viable management of the world's forests.

BOOKS IN THIS SERIES

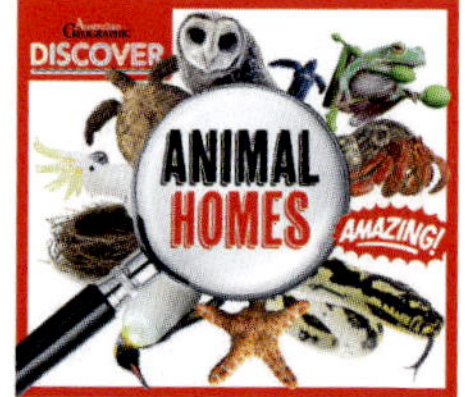

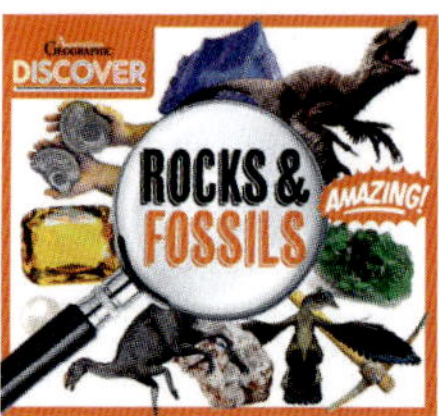

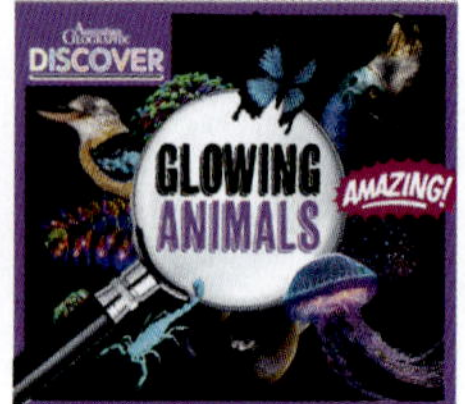

Australian Geographic contributes 100% of its profits to the Australian Geographic Society, including its conservation and sustainability programs.